Disclaimer

This book and its conte   purposes only and are n   e for any professional, me   ....., .. any other advice. In addition, the author and publisher make no representations or warranties and expressly disclaim any and all liability concerning any treatment or action by any person following the information offered or provided within or through the book. If you have specific concerns or a situation in which you require professional or medical advice, you should consult with an appropriately trained and qualified specialist.

Copyright

© 2024 Sharon Key. All rights reserved.

No part of this publication may be reproduced, distributed, or transmitted in any form or by any means, including photocopying, recording, or other electronic or mechanical methods, without prior written permission.

About the Author

Sharon Key, the heart and soul behind Just Pause, has been a beacon of tranquillity for thousands across the globe through her online mindfulness and meditation courses.

As a mindfulness meditation instructor, Sharon made the compassionate decision to open her courses to everyone amidst the Covid-19 crisis. This decision has since welcomed thousands of students worldwide into the calming embrace of her teachings.

Life presented Sharon with a formidable challenge - a rare form of lung cancer, followed by skin cancer. During this trying period, she discovered the healing power of mindfulness and meditation. These practices became her sanctuary, helping her navigate through these life-altering circumstances.

Inspired by her personal journey, Sharon thought, "As a teacher, I can make mindfulness and meditation accessible to others." And so, she did. Sharon has conducted hundreds of mindfulness meditation sessions.

When the COVID pandemic struck, she transitioned these courses online, extending her reach to aid as many individuals as possible in maintaining their mental health during these challenging times.

Part of the Awaken the Inner Calm: A Mindfulness and Meditation Series

- The Power of Mindfulness and Meditation
- Mindfulness for Children: A Practical Guide
- Mindfulness for Cancer Warriors
- Mindful Meditation Scripts

Table of Contents

Mindfulness with Cancer 6

The Healing Power of Meditation 9

Meditation: An Act of Love - Poem 11

Creating Your Sacred Meditation Space 12

Meditation Bracelet 15

Guided Meditation: A Journey Within 18

Navigating the Thought Stream 21

Navigating Life's Waters 24

Clouds in the Sky Meditation 26

Daily Mindfulness Practice 30

A, B, C Awareness 32

Embracing the Art of Waiting 35

Awakening the Senses 37

Waiting with Kindness 41

The Art of Awareness 43

The Body Scan Meditation 46

Smiling: An Infectious Light - Poem 48

Embodied Tranquillity Meditation 49

Embracing Acceptance 52

Navigating Acceptance: A Journey of 54

Healing Light Meditation 56

Letting Go 58

Crossroads of Emotion - Story 60
Mountain Meditation 62
Kindness and Patience 64
Kindness and Patience Meditation 66
Gratitude Journal 68
The Ripple of Kindness - Story 70
The Forest of Arrows - Story 73
Navigating Pain 76
Summary and Everyday Practice 79

Chapter 1

Mindfulness with Cancer

Cancer is a complex and often overwhelming experience that can trigger many emotions, such as fear, uncertainty, and emotional turbulence. People often face physical challenges, such as pain, fatigue, and nausea, as well as a variety of medical treatments, including chemotherapy, radiation, and surgery.

However, amidst the chaos and difficulty of cancer, there lies an opportunity for healing. Mindfulness, the practice of being fully present in the moment, offers patients a path toward inner peace, resilience, and emotional well-being. By focusing on the present moment and observing one's thoughts and emotions without judgment, patients can reduce stress and anxiety, cultivate a sense of calm, and develop greater self-awareness.

In addition to its emotional benefits, mindfulness has also been shown to have physical benefits for cancer patients, such as reducing pain and fatigue, improving sleep quality, and boosting the immune system. Moreover, practising mindfulness can help patients feel more in control of their bodies and lives, leading to greater feelings of empowerment and hope.

Overall, mindfulness is a valuable tool for cancer patients to help them navigate this challenging time with greater ease, resilience, and emotional well-being. It can help with:

1. **Navigating the Uncontrollable**: Many aspects of the cancer experience are beyond our control—the diagnosis, treatment protocols, and prognosis. Mindfulness invites us to shift our focus from what we cannot change to what we can: our attention and our responses.
2. **Embracing the Present**: Mindfulness encourages us to be here now. It invites us to step away from the past (with its regrets and memories) and the future (with its anxieties and uncertainties). In the present moment, we can find solace, clarity, and strength.
3. **The Mind-Body Connection**: Research shows that mindfulness practices positively impact physical health. By calming the mind, we alleviate stress, boost immunity, and enhance overall well-being.

Our thoughts and emotions influence our body's responses, and mindfulness helps us harness this connection.

Visualise your thoughts as passing clouds. Learn to observe them without judgment, allowing them to drift away. Simple practices for daily life—Awareness, Breath, Compassion. These ABCs ground you in the present moment. Plus, so much more awaits you within these pages—a journey of acceptance, resilience, and kindness. Let this book be your companion as you navigate the twists and turns of the cancer path.

The Healing Power of Meditation

Introduction

In our journey through mindfulness, we encounter a powerful ally: meditation. This ancient practice holds immense benefits for our well-being, both mentally and physically. Let's explore why meditation is a vital tool, especially when dealing with cancer.

The Many Benefits of Meditation

Relaxation and Stress Reduction: Meditation provides a sanctuary of calm amidst life's storms. By focusing our attention inward, we release tension, soothe our nerves, and find respite from the chaos around us.

Anxiety Management: The practice of meditation gently guides us away from anxiety's grip. As we breathe mindfully, our worries lose their intensity, allowing us to regain clarity and peace.

Physical Healing: When we meditate, we give our bodies a chance to heal. The quietness of meditation supports cellular repair, reduces inflammation, and supports our immune system.

Morning, Afternoon, or Evening? The choice is yours. Some prefer the serenity of morning meditation, while others find solace in the evening. Research suggests that midday meditation strikes a harmonious balance. Listen to your body's cues. If mornings find you drifting back to sleep, perhaps midday or evening sessions suit you better.

Preparation Matters: Settle into a comfortable space. Whether it's your meditation mat or the cosy corner of your sofa, make it your sanctuary.

Practice: Meditation doesn't require an audience. You can meditate anywhere—sitting, standing, or lying down. No need for grand gestures; simply find comfort.

Hospital Appointments: Facing medical appointments? Meditate beforehand. Calm your nerves, centre your mind, and step into the hospital with resilience.

Waiting Room Zen: While waiting, meditate discreetly. No one needs to know. Lower your eyes, breathe, and let stillness envelop you.

It's a gentle companion on our cancer journey, offering support, strength, and healing.

Meditation: An Act of Love - Poem

Don't meditate to please others. Instead, meditate as an act of love—a tender embrace for your soul.

To improve yourself, to redeem yourself, rather do it as an act of love. Imagine it: a warm friendship blossoming within you, like sun-kissed petals unfurling.

In this way, there is no longer any need for support. No more desperate reaching for external validation or approval. You become your own sanctuary.

A question of self-improvement. But not the kind that weighs you down with guilt—the relentless pursuit of "enough."

It offers the possibility of acceptance. The ceaseless striving, the exhausting race against your own shadow.

Instead, though, is now meditation. A quiet revolution—a rebellion against the noise.

As an act of love, you sit, cradle your breath, and listen to the symphony of your heart.

How endlessly delightful. The gentle rhythm of your pulse.

Meditate. Not to fix, but to love. Not to strive, but to embrace.

Creating Your Sacred Meditation Space

The art of crafting your own sacred meditation space—a haven where tranquillity and self-discovery intertwine.

Daily Meditation: A Gift to Yourself

First things first: daily meditation. If you can weave this practice into your life, you're already on the path to reclaiming control—control over your thoughts, emotions, and well-being. It's not about perfection; it's about consistency.

Claim Your Space

Now, let's talk about that magical corner of your world—the space where meditation unfolds. Whether it's a cosy nook or a sunlit room, find a spot that resonates with you.

Here's how:

Explore your home. Seek out that quiet alcove—the **one** where time slows down. It might be a corner of your bedroom, a sunroom, or even a cushioned chair by the window.

Personalise It:

Transform this space into your sanctuary. Add a touch of intentionality. Maybe a meditation mat awaits your presence. Perhaps a scented candle flickers or crystals. Make it yours.

The Chair or the Floor?

If the floor beckons, sit cross-legged, grounding yourself. Or a chair—just ensure it's comfortable and supportive. Remember, this is your space.

The Mindset Shift

As you step into your chosen space, a subtle shift occurs. Your mindset aligns with meditation.

Consistency:

By returning to the same spot, your mind recognises the habits. It's like a secret handshake between you and your inner calm.

Bedtime vs. Meditation Time:

The bed, but beware! Meditating there often leads to unplanned naps. Instead, reserve your bed for restful slumber. Your meditation space deserves its own spotlight.

The Conservatory of Stillness

Now, let me share my personal oasis—the conservatory. Sunlight filters through the glass, dappling the floor. Here, I sit, legs crossed, eyes closed. The world outside fades, and I'm cocooned in serenity.

This is my time. My sacred pause.

So, whether it's a sunlit conservatory, a cushion, or a corner, make it yours. Let it serve as your gateway to mindfulness.

Meditation Bracelet

Let's explore another mindfulness tool that I hold dear—the meditation bracelet. Beaded bracelets have the power to anchor us in the present moment, wherever we are.

Picture this: a simple bracelet of beads. It's unpretentious, yet its impact is profound. Here's why I recommend meditation beads to anyone seeking inner calm:

Meditation beads are like pocket-sized meditations. Slip one onto your wrist, and you're carrying peace with you. No matter the chaos that is around you, your beads are always there to help you calm down.

You don't need a specific type of bracelet. Any beaded bracelet will do. Whether it's a Mala bead or a homemade design, the magic lies in the beads themselves.

The digital marketplace is a treasure trove. Search for "Mala beads" or "Mala bracelets." You'll discover an array of options, from necklaces to bracelets.

If store-bought isn't your style, create your own. Visit a local shop, pick out beads that speak to you, and string them together. Your unique creation becomes a talisman of peace.

Now, let's dive into the heart of it—the breathing exercise with your meditation beads.

Here's how to use them:

Sit comfortably. Maybe you're on a cushion, cross-legged, or nestled in your favourite chair. Or you could be sitting in your parked car, sitting on a park bench. These can be done anywhere, anytime.

Feel the beads against your skin. Each one is a tactile reminder of presence. Let your fingers explore their texture.

As you inhale, slide a bead between your fingers. Exhale, and move to the next. Repeat. Let your breath dance with the beads. Inhale, exhale, bead by bead.

Ah, the dangling bead! It's your guide. When you reach it, pause. Reflect. Set an intention. Then, continue your rhythmic breathing.

As you breathe, eyes closed, the world fades. The bracelet focuses on your object of meditation—a bridge to stillness. And whether you're in a bustling café or your quiet corner at home, your beads whisper, "This is your time."

So wear your beads proudly, my fellow seeker. Let them be your compass, pointing inward. And when life tugs at your sleeve, touch your beads. Breathe. Come into the present moment.

Guided Meditation: A Journey Within

In the peacefulness of your sacred space, let us embark on a journey—a journey within. Find a comfortable seat, straighten your spine, and let the world outside fade away.

Sit Comfortably:

Sit in your chosen spot. Back straight, shoulders relaxed. Feel the earth supporting you. You are here.

Eyes Closed:

Close your eyes. Let the darkness envelop you. Trust that your inner vision will illuminate the way.

Stillness Descends:

Allow your body to settle. No fidgeting, no restlessness. Just stillness. Breathe.

Natural Breathing:

Notice your breath. Inhale through your nose, exhale through your mouth. No need to alter it—just witness.

The Mind's Dance:

Thoughts may pirouette across your mind's stage. When they steal your attention, gently guide it back to your breath. Inhale, exhale.

Body Sensations:

Feel your body. Any tingling, warmth, or coolness? Acknowledge these sensations—they are your companions.

The Body Scan

Begin at your crown. Imagine a soft light sweeping down, touching each part of you. Forehead, eyes, jaw, neck. Notice how your body responds.

Continue—the shoulders, chest, belly. Feel your heartbeat, the rhythm of life. Hips, thighs, knees. Each note plays in harmony.

Toes, soles, heels. You are whole. Your body whispers its secrets. Listen.

The Counting Breath

Now, let's count. Inhale—one. Exhale—two. Continue until you reach ten. Then, like a river, start anew.

Repeat!

The Return

As you breathe, your awareness expands. You're not just a body; you're the space around it. Feel the room, the air, the quiet.

Slowly, bring your attention back. Wiggle your fingers, your toes. When you are ready, open your eyes.

Chapter 2

Navigating the Thought Stream

The realm of thoughts—the unending current that flows through our minds like a swift river. Thoughts surge forth and recede, sometimes slipping beyond our grasp. Yet, take heart; we possess the ability to guide and harness them.

Countless Thoughts:

Imagine this: a bustling marketplace of ideas. You, the observer, stand in the midst of it all. Each day, you encounter a staggering **60,000 thoughts**—a carousel of mental activity.

The Mind's Whirlwind:

Thoughts whirl like footballs, ricocheting off the walls of your consciousness. Sometimes, they collide, creating a symphony of chaos. No wonder we feel like our minds are a carnival of madness.

Emotions in the Mix:

Thoughts don't travel alone; they bring emotions and feelings as companions. Worries, hopes, and anxieties ride alongside. These emotional passengers can affect our bodies, making us feel physically unwell.

Mindfulness: The Settling Jar

The Satellite Dish:

Now, picture a satellite dish. Its purpose? To settle the thought storm. Just as we can't extract thoughts from our minds, we can't remove data from the jar. But mindfulness offers a way to calm the chaos.

The Settling Process:

The jar remains full, yet the illusion of less. Mindfulness doesn't eliminate thoughts; it tames them. We regain a sense of control, like a ship steadying itself in turbulent waters.

The Breath as Anchor:

In meditation, we return to our breath—the anchor. When thoughts gallop, we gently guide our attention back. Inhale, exhale. The breath becomes our North Star.

The Illusion of Stillness

Thoughts Revisited:

Thoughts arise, but we don't ride everyone. Instead, we watch them from the riverbank. They're bubbles, eddies, fleeting clouds. Not facts, not truths—just mental events.

The Dangling Bead:

Imagine a bead dangling from your bracelet. When thoughts emerge, pause. Reflect. Set an intention. Then, return to counting breaths. The bead guides you back.

Awareness Expands:

As you breathe, your awareness expands. You're not just a thinker; you're the vast space around thoughts. Feel the room, the air, the quiet.

The jar remains full, but you perceive it differently. You're more than the thought storm. You're the stillness between.

Navigating Life's Waters

The concept of the **stress bucket** is a powerful metaphor that helps us understand how stress accumulates and affects us.

The Stress Bucket Theory

Your Personal Bucket:

Imagine a bucket—a unique vessel within you. Each person's bucket varies in size because we all handle stress differently. Yours might be small or spacious, but it's always there.

The Water of Stress:

Picture a pail of water. This water symbolises your stressors—financial worries, health concerns, family issues, and work pressures. As you encounter stress, you pour water into your bucket.

The Rising Tide:

Your bucket fills up. Financial woes add water. Health concerns contribute more. The water level rises. Family matters and work stress pour in. Soon, your bucket nears the rim.

Overflowing Buckets:

Most of us live with nearly full buckets. We teeter on the edge, unable to handle much more stress. A simple incident—a spilt drink—can tip the balance. Suddenly, the overflow spills out.

Our Reactions:

When the bucket overflows, we react. Some shout, others cry. Neither response is right or wrong; it's how we cope. But the overflow signals that we've reached our limit.

Mindful Coping Strategies:

Imagine taps on the side of your bucket. These taps represent coping strategies. When stress fills your bucket, turn on the taps. What works for you? Exercise, meditation, reading, socialising, or simply taking a break?

Reflect and Release:

Reflect on your existing coping skills. Remember moments when you managed stress effectively. Acknowledge your abilities. Use what you know to empty your bucket.

The Overflow and Breakdown

Sometimes, it's a spilled drink that pushes us over the edge. The last drop of stress causes our bucket to overflow. We break down—cry, shout, or both.

Remember:

It's OK. We're human. Our buckets have limits. Recognise when yours is overflowing. Turn on the taps. Empty it. Seek support if needed.

Your stress bucket is real. Acknowledge it. Be kind to yourself. When life spills over, remember: you're not alone. We all have buckets to manage.

Clouds in the Sky Meditation

Meditation—**Clouds in the Sky**. Find a comfortable position, whether sitting or lying down. Let's explore the ever-changing landscape of our minds, just like clouds drifting across the sky.

1. The Breath as Anchor

Sit comfortably. Straighten your spine, relax your shoulders, and close your eyes. Bring your attention to your breath—the gentle rise and fall.

Body Awareness:

Expand your awareness to your entire body. Feel your chest expand with each inhale; your belly soften with each exhale. Be present in this moment.

2. Clouds of Thought

Imagine your thoughts as clouds. They drift across the vast sky of your mind. Some are wispy, others dense. Observe them without judgment.

Thoughts come and go, just like clouds. Notice them entering your awareness, then gently floating away. No need to hold on or chase them.

3. The Still Sky

Be the sky—the spacious container for thoughts. Watch them from a distance. They're not you; they're mental events. Let them pass.

Emotions arise, too. Like storm clouds, they darken the sky. Observe their intensity. Let them sail by without clinging.

4. Return to Breath

When thoughts or emotions pull you away, return to your breath. Inhale, exhale. The breath is your anchor, grounding you.

As you breathe, notice the gaps between thoughts—the clear sky. In those spaces, find stillness and clarity.

6. The Stillness Within

As you breathe, notice the gaps between thoughts. These are the silent spaces—the clear sky. In those moments, you're not thinking; you're simply being. Embrace this stillness.

Imagine thoughts as visitors to your mind. They knock on the door, stay for a while, and then depart. Some are chatty; others are fleeting. Greet them all with curiosity.

7. The Infinite Sky

Now, expand your awareness beyond the confines of your body. Feel the room around you—the air, the walls, the floor. You're not separate from your environment; you're

Consider that your mind is like the sky—an infinite expanse. Thoughts are like passing birds. They fly in, perch on branches, and take flight again. You remain in the vast sky.

8. The Compassionate Observer

As you observe thoughts, be kind to yourself. Don't judge their content. Instead, notice how they make you feel. Are they heavy or light? Allow them to be without resistance.

Sometimes, thoughts carry messages. They remind you of tasks, dreams, or memories. Acknowledge their purpose. Then, let them continue their journey across the sky of your mind.

9. The Return to Breath

Return to your breath—the ever-present anchor. Inhale, exhale. Feel the rise and fall. It's here, in this rhythm, that you find stability.

Thank your mind for its ceaseless activity. It's a loyal companion, even when it feels chaotic. Like a faithful dog, it follows you everywhere. Embrace its quirks.

Chapter 3

Daily Mindfulness Practice

The power of daily mindfulness practice—a gentle yet transformative journey that can enrich your life. Whether you're a seasoned practitioner or just starting out, weaving mindfulness into your daily routine can yield remarkable benefits.

1. The Art of Consistency

Imagine mindfulness as a daily companion—a loyal friend who walks beside you. To truly make a difference, we must embrace it consistently. Like tending to a garden, mindfulness flourishes with regular care.

Scientists recommend dedicating **10 to 20 minutes** each day to mindfulness. Within this pocket of time, you can reduce stress, anxiety, and depression by up to **60 percent**. It's a small investment with profound returns.

2. Tips for Daily Practice

Infuse mindfulness into your daily life. Notice the sensations of your morning coffee, the breeze on your skin during a lunchtime walk, or the warmth of your bed at night. Each moment is an opportunity to be present.

You don't need to meditate for hours. **One minute here, two minutes there**—these micro-moments add up. Pause, breathe, and reconnect with the present. It's like sprinkling seeds of mindfulness throughout your day.

3. The Magic of Meditation

Meditation is your sacred space—a quiet refuge where you meet yourself. Aim for consistency. Even **one minute** of focused meditation can anchor your day.

Break the mould. Meditate during your commute, while waiting in line, or before bedtime. It's not about duration; **it's about intention. Let meditation ripple through your day.**

4. The Ripple Effect

Mindfulness isn't confined to your meditation cushion. It spills into your interactions, your choices, and your reactions. As you practice, notice how it colours your world.

Weave mindfulness into your daily fabric. When stress knocks, breathe mindfully. When joy visits, savour it fully. Each moment is a thread in your tapestry of awareness.

A, B, C Awareness

A simple yet powerful mindfulness technique that you can incorporate into your daily life. Whether you're at home, waiting for appointments, or feeling wound up, this practice is accessible anytime, anywhere. I call it the **A, B, C Awareness**—a way to anchor yourself in the present moment.

The A, B, C Steps

Attend to Your Surroundings:

Pause. Look around. Notice what's happening in your environment. Engage all your senses:

- What do you see? Colours, shapes, textures.
- What do you hear? Sounds, whispers, rustling leaves.
- What do you smell? Scents, fragrances, the air.
- What do you feel? Temperature, textures, sensations.

- What do you taste? Flavours, remnants of your last meal.

Reconnect with the world outside your head. You're here now.

B: Be in Your Body:

- Shift your attention inward. Feel your physical presence:
- If sitting, notice your feet on the floor. Shoes against your skin.
- Weight distribution—bum on the chair, pressure on your toes.
- Temperature—warm or cool sensations.
- If lying down, feel the bed's support. Even weight distribution.
- Any pain? Breathe kindness into that area on the out-breath.

C: Cultivate Kindness:

- As you breathe, infuse kindness into your body:
- Inhale: Kindness flows to any discomfort.
- Exhale: Relax and release tension.
- No judgment—just gentle awareness and care.

Grounding in the Present:

A, B, and C bring you back to the present moment. It's like adjusting the lens of your awareness.

Amid life's chaos, find stillness in these simple steps.

Daily Integration:

- Use it during routine moments:
- Waiting for your morning coffee.
- Sitting in a meeting.
- Lying down for rest.
- Accumulate these mindful micro-moments throughout your day.

A, B, C, Awareness is your compass—a way to navigate the currents of life. As you practice, remember you're both the observer and the observed.

Chapter 4

Embracing the Art of Waiting

The art of waiting—a space where time stretches and uncertainty looms. Whether you're awaiting test results, medical appointments, or life-changing decisions, waiting can be a challenging mental landscape. But fear not; mindfulness and meditation can be your companions during these moments of anticipation.

1. The Weight of Waiting

The Long Months:

Waiting for a diagnosis can feel like an eternity. Ten months—an intricate dance between hope and fear. Rare cancers demand patience, resilience, and unwavering strength.

The Mental Strain:

Waiting isn't just about calendars and clocks; it's a mental marathon. Thoughts race—scenarios unfold. Google becomes both ally and adversary, offering answers and horror stories alike.

2. The Mindfulness Sanctuary

Daily Practice:

- Amid the waiting, embrace mindfulness. It's not a shortcut; it's a daily practice. Spend a few minutes each day:
- **Noticing the Present:** Observe your surroundings—the colours, sounds, and textures. You're here now.
- **Being in Your Body:** Feel your feet on the floor, the chair supporting you. Acknowledge any discomfort with kindness.
- **Breathing Kindness:** Inhale compassion for any pain; exhale relaxation.

Art as Meditation:

When physical activity is limited, turn to art. Sketch, paint, or create. Let your mind rest from its relentless chatter. Art becomes your mindful exercise—a break from the waiting.

3. The Mindful Pause

- Google offers information overload—both solace and dread. Mindfulness, on the other hand, invites you to pause:
- **Reflect on Breath:** When thoughts spiral, return to your breath. Inhale, exhale. You're here, not in the future's maze.
- **Release the Stories:** Thoughts are clouds; they pass. Let go of worst-case scenarios. They don't define you.

The Canvas of Now:

Waiting isn't empty time; it's a canvas. Paint it with presence. Notice the brush strokes—the colours of your emotions, the texture of your resilience.

Awakening the Senses

The world of our five senses—a gateway to mindfulness. These senses are our anchors to the present moment, pulling us away from the whirlwind of thoughts and worries. By engaging our senses intentionally, we can savour life's richness and find solace in the now.

1. The Five Senses Pathway

Seeing Clearly:

Look around. Notice colours, shapes, and textures. What catches your eye? The world unfolds before you, and you're here to witness it. Let your gaze be a reminder to be present.

Tasting Mindfully:

Take a bite. Savour it. Feel the texture, the flavours dancing on your tongue. Each taste is a portal to the present. You can't truly taste unless you're fully here.

Feeling the World:

Touch an object. Is it soft or hard? Warm or cool? Your fingertips connect you to reality. Let touch be your guide back to now.

Listening Attentively:

Close your eyes. Listen. Birds, traffic, distant laughter—they're all part of this moment. Your ears are the gatekeepers to presence. Tune in.

Inhaling Aromas:

Breathe in. Smell the coffee, the flowers, the rain-soaked earth. Aromas weave stories of now. Let your nose lead you home.

2. The Mindful Walk

Birdsong Symphony:

Go for a walk. Listen to the birds. Their melodies pull you out of your mind. You're not just walking; you're dancing with the present.

Petrichor Perfume:

After the rain, smell the earth. Petrichor—the scent of wet soil—grounds you. Inhale deeply. You're part of this cycle.

3. The Pause Button

Sensory Breaks:

Throughout your day, pause. Use your senses:

- **See:** Notice the details around you.
- **Taste:** Sip your tea mindfully.
- **Touch:** Feel the texture of your desk.
- **Listen:** Birds, laughter, silence.
- **Smell:** Breathe in life's fragrances.

These mini-breaks reset your mind.

The Present Invitation:

When worry knocks, open the door to your senses. They'll usher you back to now. Your mind is a guest; don't let it take over the house.

Your senses are the compass needles pointing to presence. Use them generously.

Chapter 5

Waiting with Kindness

Take a moment. Breathe. You're here, in this waiting room of life. Let's practice kindness—kindness to yourself, to your racing thoughts, to the uncertainty that hangs in the air.

1. The Breath as Anchor

Three Deep Breaths:

Inhale deeply. Feel your chest expand. Exhale fully. Let go of tension. Repeat this three times. You're grounding yourself.

Normal Rhythm:

Return to your natural breath. It's your constant companion—the rhythm of life. Notice it without **judgment.**

2. The Mantra of Compassion

May I Be Well:

- Whisper these words to yourself:
- "May I be well?"
- "In the midst of waiting, may I be peaceful?"
- "Even in uncertainty, may I be safe and protected?"

Let them settle within you. Imagine your kindest friend speaking to you.

Your Special Phrase:

Choose a phrase that resonates with you. Repeat it silently when anxiety knocks. It's your lifeline back to now.

3. The Return to Breath

Breath Awareness:

As thoughts swirl, return to your breath. Inhale, exhale. It's your anchor—a gentle reminder that you're here, not lost in the labyrinth of what-ifs.

Eyes Open:

When you're ready, open your eyes. The room looks different now. You've infused it with kindness.

The Art of Awareness

Let's explore the heart of mindfulness: **awareness**. It's the compass that guides us back to the present moment. As we journey together, we'll delve into our bodies, practising the **art of noticing and feeling. Are you ready? Let's begin.**

1. The Essence of Mindfulness

Mindfulness whispers, "Be here." It's about noticing—both the outer world and the inner landscape. Imagine your senses as open doors, inviting you to step into the now.

The Dance of Feelings:

How do you feel? Not just the surface emotions but the subtle currents beneath. Acknowledge them. They're part of your story.

So, for example, when I feel happy, I feel like I have a smile on my face and a warmth in my heart. I feel like I can do anything, and I want to share my joy with others. I feel like my body is relaxed and comfortable. That's how happiness feels for me. But it might be different for you. You might feel happy in a different way.

And when I feel calm, I feel like I have a clear mind and a peaceful soul. I feel like I can breathe deeply and slowly. I feel like my body is still and quiet. That's how calmness feels for me. But it might be different for you. You might feel calm in a different way, and when I feel angry, I feel like I have a fire in my chest and a tightness in my throat. I feel like I can't control my emotions, and I want to lash out at others. I feel like my body is tense and rigid. That's how anger feels for me. But it might be different for you. You might feel angry in a different way.

And when I feel sad, I feel like I have a weight on my shoulders and a lump in my stomach. I feel like I can't see the bright side, and I want to cry. I feel like my body is heavy and sluggish. That's how sadness feels for me. But it might be different for you. You might feel sad in a different way.

And when I feel stressed, I feel like I have pressure in my head and a knot in my back. I feel like I can't cope with everything, and I want to escape. I feel like my body is restless and agitated. That's how stress feels for me. But it might be different for you. You might feel stressed in a different way.

So, by noticing how different emotions feel in our body, we can become more aware of ourselves and our feelings. We can also learn to manage them better and prevent them from becoming too overwhelming. We can use different strategies to cope with different emotions, such as breathing exercises, positive affirmations, mindfulness, or talking to someone. We can also try to cultivate more positive emotions, such as gratitude, compassion, and happiness, by doing things that make us feel good, such as hobbies, exercise, or spending time with loved ones. By doing this, we can improve our well-being and our quality of life.

The Body Scan Meditation

Body as Canvas:

Close your eyes. Breathe. Imagine your body as a canvas. We'll paint it with awareness, stroke by stroke.

Systematic Exploration:

Start at your toes. Feel them—tingling, grounded. Move upward: feet, ankles, calves. Notice tension. Release it. Continue: knees, thighs, hips. Each part whispers its story.

The Spine's Tale:

Your spine—a bridge between heaven and earth. Feel its curves, its strength. It carries you. Honour it.

Shoulders and Neck:

Release burdens. Let your shoulders drop. Unclench your jaw. Breathe into your neck. It cradles your head—the seat of wisdom.

The Crown Jewel:

Your head—a universe of sensations. Forehead, temples, ears. Feel them. You're alive.

3. The Return to Breath

Anchor in Breath:

Open your eyes. Breathe. Your breath—the eternal companion. Inhale, exhale. It's your ticket to presence.

Smiling: An Infectious Light - Poem

Smiling, a sunbeam in disguise, Infectious as laughter, swift as butterflies. Catch it like a melody, a sweet refrain. When someone smiles, a chain reaction begins.

Around the corner, a stranger's eyes alight. My grin reflected, and a spark ignited. He smiles back, a silent pact we share. A ripple of joy dances through the air.

I ponder that smile, its quiet power, A currency of kindness, hour by hour. A single smile, a currency so rare, Could circumnavigate the globe, I swear.

So if you feel a smile, don't hesitate. Let it bloom, uncontained, radiate. Invisible but potent, it spreads undetected, An epidemic of light, hearts reconnected.

Let's infect the world with grins and glee, A revolution of joy, wild and free. For in this simple act, we find our worth, Smiling—our universal language of mirth.

Embodied Tranquillity Meditation

Find a comfortable position, a sanctuary for your body and mind. Let's embark on a journey of relaxation—a voyage within. Close your eyes if it feels right, or soften your gaze. Breathe. We'll explore each corner of your being, one breath at a time.

Breath as Your Anchor

Notice your breath. Inhale, exhale. No need to alter it—simply observe. Your breath is your compass, guiding you back to now.

Feet Grounded:

Shift your attention to your feet. Tighten the muscles there. Feel the tension. Then, on your next exhale, release. Let your feet melt into the chair or floor.

Calf Muscles and Shins:

Move upward. Calves and shins. Tighten. Hold. Then, like a sigh, let go. Feel the relaxation seep through your legs.

Thighs and Hips

Thighs and hips—your sturdy foundation. Contract those muscles. Sense the strength. Hold. Now, as you exhale, surrender. Sink deeper into the chair, into presence.

Back and Spine:

Your spine—a bridge between worlds. Notice its curves, its resilience. Breathe into your back. It carries stories, memories, and dreams.

Shoulders and Chest

Shoulders—gatekeepers of tension. Lift them toward your ears. Hold. Then, like petals falling, release. Feel the weightlessness.

Chest Expanding:

Chest rising with each breath. Inhale, exhale. Your heart dances within. Let it sway to the rhythm of now.

Hips and Belly

Hips and pelvis—your centre of gravity. Tighten. Hold. Then, like a river finding its course, release. Feel the flow.

Belly Breathing:

Place your hand on your belly. Inhale, let it rise. Exhale, let it fall. Your breath massages your core. You're alive.

Back and Spine (Again)

Return to your spine. Its wisdom whispers. Each vertebra is a chapter. Breathe into its pages.

Full Body Awareness:

Expand your awareness. Feet to head. You're a symphony of sensations. Breathe. You're here.

Chapter 6

Embracing Acceptance

In this sacred space, let's explore the art of acceptance—a path strewn with emotions, resilience, and quiet strength. When life hands us a diagnosis like cancer, we grapple with a whirlwind of feelings. Denial, anger, and bargaining dance around us, each demanding its moment in the spotlight. But acceptance—the quiet hero—awaits its turn.

1. The Stages of Grief

Denial's Veil:

When I first heard the words "heart-lung cancer," my mind recoiled. I'd never smoked, yet here I was, facing an unfair battle. Denial wrapped me in its cold embrace. "Not me," I whispered. But reality seeped through the cracks.

Anger's Fire:

Anger followed swiftly. Who could I blame? Cancer doesn't play favourites. No one to point fingers at—just a silent adversary. I carried that anger, a smouldering ember, for weeks. Why me? Why now?

2. The Courage to Accept

The Unwanted Guest:

Acceptance isn't surrender. It's acknowledging the uninvited guest in your life. Cancer, like an unwelcome visitor, settles in. It doesn't mean you wanted it; it means you're ready to face it.

The Dialogue Within:

Acceptance quiets the inner turmoil. No more wrestling with guilt or bargaining with fate. It's saying, "This is my reality." Not resignation but a stepping stone toward action.

3. The Energy Shift

From Wishing to Fighting:

By accepting, you reclaim your energy. Redirect it from futile wishes to purposeful battles. Cancer isn't your choice, but how you respond is. Spend time with loved ones. Seek treatment. Live fiercely.

The Family of Emotions:

Acceptance doesn't erase anger or fear. It invites them to sit at the table. They're part of your emotional family. Acknowledge them, but don't let them dictate your journey.

4. The Healing Power of Acceptance

A Quiet Hero:

Acceptance isn't flashy. It doesn't scream for attention. But it heals. It whispers, "You're not alone." It allows you to breathe to find solace in the present.

Acceptance isn't defeat. It's a bridge to resilience. You're not giving up; you're stepping forward.

Navigating Acceptance: A Journey of

Acceptance, the silent companion on our journey, doesn't shout; it whispers. When life delivers a cancer diagnosis, we fight with emotions—fear, anger, and vulnerability.

The Permission to Not Be OK: Acceptance isn't an easy thing to do. "It's OK not to be OK." Cancer isn't a welcome guest; it barges in uninvited. We wrestle with shock, denial, and disbelief.

The Avalanche of Thoughts

When I received my cancer diagnosis, I felt powerless—incapable of movement, unable to watch television without tears. Yet, in that fragile moment, acceptance whispered, "It's OK not to be OK."

Perfection isn't a prerequisite for acceptance. It doesn't follow a linear path. Instead, it involves stumbling, falling, and then rising again. You don't have to be strong all the time; sometimes, it's OK to unravel.

Emotional Scale

Imagine a scale from 1 to 10. At level 1, you're brilliant—coping, thriving. But when life strikes, you might soar to level 9. Acceptance gently says, "It's OK." You're not failing; you're human.

At level 9, vulnerability reigns. Tears flow, and that's OK. You're dealing with a lot, and that's OK, too.

The Quiet Strength Within

Acceptance isn't defeat; it's resilience. It acknowledges, "I see you cancer. I won't pretend." It's OK not to be OK. Allow yourself to slowly accept that this is what you have, and moments become more manageable.

Healing Light Meditation

Find a comfortable position and start to relax. If it feels right, close your eyes. Let's embark on a healing journey.

1. Breath as Your Guide

Awareness of Breath:

Breathe. Inhale, exhale. No need to alter it; simply observe. Your breath—the rhythm of life. Feel its gentle rise and fall.

Counted Breaths:

Inhale to the count of three. Hold. Exhale to the count of three. Repeat. Inhale, two, three. Exhale, two, three. Let this rhythm anchor you.

2. Green Healing Light

Pure Green Energy:

Imagine a radiant green light. It's healing and soothing. Picture it filling your entire body—from your crown to your toes. Feel its warmth, its vibrancy.

Healing Touch:

With each breath, draw in this green energy. Let it flow to any part of your body that needs healing. Imagine it soothing tension, melting away discomfort.

Relaxation and Renewal:

As you breathe, this healing light relaxes you. It whispers, "You're safe." It allows your body to mend to find balance.

3. Releasing the Darkness

Exhaling Negativity:

Now, imagine exhaling grey, dark energy. Release it with each breath. Let it dissolve into the air. You're shedding what no longer serves you.

Letting Go of Worry:

As you exhale, let go of worries, fears, and illness. They dissipate like smoke. You're making space for healing.

4. The Healing Margin

Green Energy Embrace:

Continue this dance. Inhale green light, exhale darkness. Feel the margin of healing expanding within you.

Letting Go

The art of letting go—one of the seven attitudes of mindfulness. How does this relate to your cancer journey? Let's unravel it together.

1. The Weight of Expectations

Uncharted Paths:

Letting go isn't easy. It takes many forms. Perhaps you're releasing the life you thought you'd have. Or maybe it's the image of your body—the one you once knew.

Hair and Identity:

Losing hair through chemotherapy—it's a silent struggle. You look different. It's OK to mourn that loss. Your reflection changes, but your essence remains.

2. The Guilt We Carry

The Uninvited Guest:

Guilt—like an unwelcome visitor—settles in. Why me? Why now? You're not alone. Many feel guilty for putting their family and friends through the stress and worry of a loved one who has cancer.

The Weight of Blame:

Cancer isn't your fault. Experts don't fully understand why most types develop. Sometimes, we blame lifestyle choices. But let go of past mistakes. Forgive yourself and others.

3. The Healing Path

Acceptance and Release:

Letting go improves well-being. Guilt will ebb and flow. Share your feelings with someone you trust. Join a support group. Focus on gratitude. Find healthy ways to express emotions.

The Imperfect Dance:

You're not alone in this labyrinth. Letting go isn't defeat; it's resilience. You're not giving up; you're making space for healing.

Crossroads of Emotion - Story

In the quiet corners of life, we encounter moments that shape us. Let's explore two scenarios—a fork in the road where emotions collide.

Scenario One: The Rushing Friend

You're feeling low. Perhaps you've just had a heated argument with someone. The air around you is heavy with unresolved tension. And then, unexpectedly, you see a friend in the street. But they rush past you, barely acknowledging your presence. Their hurried steps echo a silent message: "Can't stop now."

Your Thoughts:

- Why are they in such a hurry?
- Did I do something wrong?
- Maybe they're preoccupied with their own troubles.

Your Feelings:

- Disappointment.
- Loneliness.
- A pang of rejection.

Scenario Two: The Joyful Encounter

You're feeding on happiness. Good news has wrapped itself around your heart. You've just spent quality time with friends, laughter weaving through the air. And then, another friend rushes past you in the street. They're in a hurry, barely pausing to say hello.

Your Thoughts:

- Why are they so busy?
- Did they not notice my joy?
- Maybe they're caught up in their own world.

Your Feelings:

- Surprise.
- A touch of hurt.
- A flicker of confusion.

In these fleeting moments, we glimpse the complexity of human connections. Our emotions dance, intersecting and diverging. Life unfolds, and we stand at the crossroads—wondering, feeling, and seeking meaning. **Which path will you choose?**

Mountain Meditation

Find a quiet space where the world's clamour fades. Sit with your back straight, head held high. Close your eyes and breathe.

The Mountain's Presence

Steadfast and Dignified:

Imagine yourself as a mountain. Your spine—its sturdy core. Shoulders relax, hands resting on your knees. You sit with dignity, a resolve etched into your bones.

Wholeness Unfolding:

Feel complete. You're not fragmented; you're whole. As you breathe, sense the mountain's presence within you.

The Mountain's Form

Visualise the Summit:

Picture the most magnificent mountain you've ever seen. It stands tall, its peak touching the sky. Notice its shape—perhaps an oval, a gentle slope, or multiple peaks.

Solidity and Beauty:

Observe its massiveness, its solidity. From afar, it's majestic, up close, intricate. Maybe snow crowns its peak; trees cling to its slopes. It's both grand and intimate.

Becoming the Mountain

Rooted and Uplifted:

Bring the mountain into your body. You're sitting on its base, your head at its peak. Your shoulders and arms—the mountain's sides. Your legs—its rooted foundation.

Stillness and Resolve:

Feel the mountain's stillness. It whispers, "You're here." Your spine, its spine. Breathe. Resolve flows through you.

The Mountain's Breath

Inhale, Exhale:

Breathe. Inhale the mountain's essence. Exhale any tension. You're part of its grandeur.

The Mountain Within:

As you sit, you share in its stillness. You're not separate; you're the mountain—rooted, uplifted.

Kindness and Patience

The profound impact of kindness and patience toward yourself and others during the challenging journey of cancer. Whether you're a patient or a caregiver, these qualities can be your guiding stars.

1. Kindness to Yourself

A Compassionate Lens:

Treat yourself with kindness. Understand that your body and mind are navigating uncharted waters. It's OK not to feel 100% all the time. Be patient with your limitations.

Balancing Act:

Kindness doesn't mean pushing yourself relentlessly. Some days, doing nothing is an act of self-care. Listen to your body and honour its needs.

2. Kindness to Others

Empathy and Understanding:

Extend kindness to fellow travellers—the patients, caregivers, and healthcare providers. Everyone is fighting their own battle. A simple smile or a heartfelt word can make a difference.

Patience with Loved Ones:

Understand that your loved ones may struggle, too. They might not always know the right words or actions. Be patient with their imperfections.

3. The Healing Power of Kindness

A Ripple Effect:

Kindness isn't just a one-time gesture; it's a ripple that spreads. When you're kind to yourself, you create space for healing. When you're kind to others, you strengthen bonds.

Kindness and patience are your allies.

Chapter 7

Kindness and Patience Meditation

The healing power of kindness and patience in this moment. Find a quiet space where the world's clamour fades. Sit comfortably, your spine erect, your head held high. Close your eyes and breathe.

1. Kindness to Yourself

Body Awareness:

Notice your body. If you're sitting, feel the chair supporting you. If standing, your feet connect with the floor. If lying down, your body rests on the bed. Sense the weight, the softness, the warmth.

Kindness Mantra:

- Repeat these words to yourself:
- May I be safe in the midst of fear?
- May my treatment be helpful in the midst of illness.
- May I be peaceful in the midst of anxiety?

- *Customise* them to resonate with your heart.

Kindness to Others

Compassion Ripples:

- Extend kindness beyond yourself. Imagine everyone receiving treatment at this moment. Whisper:
- May we all be safe in the midst of fear.
- May all our treatments be helpful in the midst of illness?
- May we all be peaceful in the midst of anxiety.

Breath as Your Anchor:

- Return your attention to your breath. Inhale, exhale. Each breath is a gift—a moment of patience. Let it flow naturally.

The Healing Pause:

- Patience isn't waiting; it's a healing pause. As you breathe, allow patience to cradle you. You're not rushing; you're being.

Gratitude Journal

Welcome. Today, let's explore the transformative power of gratitude. Life is a tapestry woven with moments—some vibrant, others muted. Amidst it all, gratitude threads its way, connecting us to joy and resilience.

The Art of Gratitude

Daily Reflections:

Imagine an e-book—a sanctuary for your thoughts. Within its pages lies a gratitude journal. Each day, you'll pen down three things you're grateful for. Simple, yet profound.

Morning or Night?

Mornings bring restlessness for some—a tangle of dreams and worries. If that's you, write your gratitude list in the morning. If nights are your battleground, let gratitude be your lullaby.

The Ripple Effect

Kindness to Self:

Gratitude isn't just about saying "thank you." It's a mirror reflecting back your blessings. When you wake up feeling low, write down what you're grateful for. It shifts your focus.

A Sleep Elixir:

At night, when worries dance, gratitude becomes your sleep potion. Fill your journal with moments of grace. Let it cradle you into a restful slumber.

The Three Blessings

Your Gratitude Trio:

What are you thankful for today? It needn't be grand—a cosy home, family laughter, lost friends remembered. Write them down. Three blessings—a simple ritual with profound impact.

The Journey Begins:

Starting may feel like lifting a boulder. But once you begin, you'll discover an abundance of gratitude. It's like finding hidden treasures in everyday moments.

The Ripple of Kindness - Story

In the bustling city, where hurried footsteps echo through crowded streets, there exists a quiet tale—a tale of kindness. It begins with a taxi driver, a man who navigates the labyrinth of New York City's streets day after day. His name is Sam, and he wears his years like a well-worn coat.

One chilly evening, as the sun dipped below the skyline, Sam picked up his last fare. The address led him to an old apartment building, its walls whispering secrets of bygone days. He honked the horn, waited, and honked again. A frail voice answered, "Just a minute."

The door creaked open, revealing a woman in her nineties. She wore a print dress and a pillbox hat with a veil pinned on it, like a character from a 1940s movie. By her side stood a small nylon suitcase. The apartment, frozen in time, held memories and dust-covered furniture.

"Would you carry my bag out to the car?" she asked. Sam obliged, then assisted her slowly to the curb. She thanked him, her eyes reflecting gratitude. "It's nothing," he replied. "I try to treat my passengers the way I'd want my mother to be treated."

As they rode, she shared her address and requested a detour through downtown. "It's not the shortest way," Sam warned. "Oh, I don't mind," she said. "Take your time."

They drove through the city's heart, neon lights casting a warm glow. The woman gazed out, lost in memories. "You know," she said, "I haven't been downtown in years. My husband used to take me here. We'd dance at the old ballroom."

Sam listened, weaving through traffic. When they reached her destination, she paid the fare and added, "You've been kind. May I ask one more favour? Could you wait a moment?"

She disappeared into a nearby building, returning with a small bouquet of flowers. "These are for you," she said. "My husband loved flowers. He'd bring them home every Friday."

Sam accepted the flowers, touched by her gesture. "Thank you," he said. "You've made an old man's night."

As she shuffled away, Sam realised that kindness wasn't just a fare or a tip—it was a bridge connecting lives. He drove off, the scent of flowers filling the cab. That night, he slept with a smile, knowing that in a city of strangers, he'd shared a moment of warmth.

And so, the ripple of kindness spread—from Sam to the woman, from the woman to her late husband's memory, and perhaps even farther. In the quiet of the night, the city whispered its gratitude.

Remember, dear traveller, kindness isn't a grand gesture; it's a collection of small moments. Each one adds weight to the scale of humanity. So, as you navigate life's streets, be the taxi driver who waits, the woman who offers flowers, and the stranger who smiles. Breathe. Trust. Be.

Chapter 8

The Forest of Arrows - Story

In a distant land, nestled within the ancient Forest of Arrows, there lived a young warrior named Aria. Aria was renowned for her courage and her skill with the bow. Her arrows flew true, piercing the hearts of her enemies and protecting her people.

One day, as Aria patrolled the forest's edge, she felt a sudden, sharp pain in her shoulder—a bandit's arrow had found its mark. The physical agony seared through her, but she gritted her teeth and pulled the arrow free. That was the first arrow—the primary pain, unavoidable and immediate.

Yet, as Aria clutched her wounded shoulder, another arrow struck—an invisible one, crafted not of wood and steel but of thoughts and emotions. This second arrow was different. It whispered in her mind, weaving tales of doom and despair. "What if the wound festers? What if I can no longer wield my bow? What if I fail to protect my people?"

Aria's brow furrowed. She knew this second arrow well—the secondary pain. It wasn't the wound itself that tormented her; it was the stories she spun around it. The fear, the doubt, the imagined catastrophes—they were the true source of suffering.

Determined to understand, Aria sought out the forest's wise sage, an old woman named Elara. Elara sat beneath an ancient oak; her eyes crinkled with age and insight.

"Aria," Elara said, "you carry two arrows—the first strikes your flesh, the second your soul. The first is inevitable; it is life's pain. But the second—the stories you tell yourself—that is where suffering blooms."

"But how do I stop the second arrow?" Aria asked.

Elara smiled. "Mindfulness, my dear. When the first arrow pierces you, breathe. Feel the pain fully, but resist adding layers of fear and worry. Notice the mind's chatter—the 'what ifs' and 'maybes.'"

Aria nodded. "And if I catch myself weaving those stories?"

"Choose compassion," Elara advised. "Place your hand on your heart. Say, 'This is pain. It's OK.' Rate your acceptance—on a scale of one to ten. Then, gently increase it. You'll find that suffering lessens."

And so, Aria practised. When the next arrow struck—a bee sting, a betrayal, a loss—she breathed, felt, and observed her mind. Slowly, she untangled the second arrow's grip. The forest whispered its secrets—the pain was real, but suffering was optional.

Years passed, and Aria became not only a skilled archer but also a wise teacher. She shared the tale of the two arrows with her people, urging them to recognise their own suffering. And in that recognition, they found freedom.

So, dear reader, when life's arrows strike, remember Aria and Elara. Be mindful of that second arrow—the one you shoot yourself. For in that awareness lies the path to peace amidst pain.

Navigating Pain

Do you find yourself in a daily battle with pain? Is your mind often filled with thoughts, fears, frustrations, or confusion? Do you feel rushed and disconnected from your body? **Mindfulness** offers a calmer way to live life despite experiencing pain.

Primary Pain (First Arrow):

Definition: Primary pain arises directly from illness, injury, or damage to the body or nervous system. It's the raw information sent by the body to the brain.

- Examples: Physical injuries, surgical wounds, chronic conditions, headaches, etc.
- **Acceptance**: We can't always eliminate primary pain, but we can learn to accept it as part of life.

Secondary Pain (Second Arrow):

Definition: Secondary pain is our mind's reaction to primary pain. It often intensifies and prolongs suffering.

- **Examples**: Emotional distress, anxiety, fear, depression, and other negative feelings triggered by the primary pain.

- **Mindfulness Approach**: We can modify and reduce secondary suffering through mindfulness.
- **Body Scan**: A powerful mindfulness exercise involves scanning your body, observing sensations, and accepting them without judgment.
- **Acceptance**: Rather than resisting or fighting the pain, we learn to be with it, observe it, and breathe through it.
- **Non-**Judgmental **Awareness**: We notice where our mind goes (e.g., worry, fear) and gently return our focus to the present moment.
- **Relaxation Response**: Mindfulness induces a relaxation response, which can ease discomfort.

Mindfulness Techniques for Pain Management:

- Body Scan: Lie down, focus on each body part, and observe sensations without judgment.
- Mindful Breathing: Pay attention to your breath, allowing it to anchor you in the present.
- Mindful Activities: Engage fully in activities you enjoy, immersing yourself in the present moment.
- Self-Compassion: Be kind to yourself, acknowledging pain without self-criticism.

- Emotional Flexibility: Observe emotions without getting entangled in them.
- Acceptance: Recognise that pain will ease and that secondary suffering is optional.

Remember, mindfulness doesn't eliminate primary pain, but it transforms our relationship with it. By practising mindfulness, we can reduce suffering even when the pain remains unchanged.

Chapter 9

Summary and Everyday Practice

Congratulations on your exploration of mindfulness! As we wrap up your book, let's summarise the key insights and discuss how to integrate mindfulness into your daily life.

Summary of Key Concepts

1. **The Healing Power of Meditation:** Meditation is a gateway to inner peace and self-awareness. It allows us to connect with our true essence and find solace amidst life's challenges.

2. **Creating Your Sacred Space:** Designate a quiet corner or room where you can meditate regularly. Infuse it with positive energy and intention.

3. **Guided Meditation:** Embark on inner journeys through guided meditation. Explore your mind, emotions, and sensations with curiosity and compassion.

4. **Mindfulness in Daily Life:** Extend mindfulness beyond formal practice. Be present during routine activities—cooking, cleaning, walking—and savour each moment.

5. **Embracing Acceptance:** Acknowledge reality without denial. Acceptance doesn't mean resignation; it empowers us to respond wisely.

6. **Kindness and Patience:** Cultivate kindness toward yourself and others. Patience is a gentle companion on your journey. **Gratitude Journal**: Capture moments of joy and resilience. Gratitude magnifies positivity.

7. **Morning Ritual**: Begin your day mindfully. Take a few conscious breaths, set an intention, and express gratitude.

8. **A, B, C Awareness**: Throughout the day, pause and notice:
    - **A:** Awareness of your surroundings (sights, sounds, smells).

- B: Be in your body (sensations, posture).
- C: Cultivate Kindness: Your thoughts and emotions (without judgment).

9. **Waiting with Kindness**: When waiting (in queues, traffic), practice patience. Breathe and observe.

10. **Mountain Meditation:** Imagine yourself as a majestic mountain—steady, unshaken by passing clouds (thoughts and emotions).

11. **Kindness Meditation:** Send kind wishes to yourself and others. May all beings be happy, healthy, and at peace.

12. **Body Scan Meditation:** Regularly scan your body from head to toe. Notice the tension and release it.

13. **Gratitude Journal:** Write down three things you're grateful for each day.

Remember, mindfulness is a lifelong journey. Be patient with yourself, embrace imperfections, and celebrate small victories. May your path be filled with awareness, compassion, and inner light.

Remember that mindfulness is not a destination but a journey. It's about making a commitment to live more fully in the present moment each and every day. As you continue your mindfulness practice, may you find greater peace, joy, and fulfilment in your life.

www.justpause.co.uk

I'm grateful for the time you've spent delving into the pages of this book. Your engagement is truly appreciated.

Part of the Awaken the Inner Calm: A Mindfulness and Meditation Series

- The Power of Mindfulness and Meditation
- Mindfulness for Children: A Practical Guide
- Mindfulness for Cancer Warriors
- Mindful Meditation Scripts